Swings and Roundabouts

Developing faith as a young person

Sharon Jackson

Kevin
Mayhew

First published in 1998 by
KEVIN MAYHEW LTD
Rattlesden
Bury St Edmunds
Suffolk IP30 0SZ

0 1 2 3 4 5 6 7 8 9

ISBN 1 84003 179 4
Catalogue No 1500204

Cover illustration by Kirstie Whiteford
Cover design by Jaquetta Sergeant
Edited by David Gatward
Printed and bound in Great Britain

CONTENTS

For Grandma, Grandad
and Uncle Geoff.
With Love.

ACKNOWLEDGEMENTS

Another big thank you to everyone I thanked last time, especially to my family and friends who continue to give me support and love. Big thanks also go to:

Davy Gee: My HP. 'The earth smells sweeter after rain.' Thanks for holding that brolly! (We 'Still Remain(s).')

Lynn Jagger: I learnt so much from you. God shines through you more than you will ever know.

'The Girls': Nicky, Lorraine, Elle, Emma and Lynda. I'm still 'Faliraki Dreaming' and gutted that I won't be with you this year. Love you all! PS: 'I can see the pub from 'ere!'

Anna Weatherley: Very long time no see, but I couldn't forget you. You're still a special friend.

Sheila Russell: 'The voice'. I spent so many choir practices stood next to you in the hope that your talent may rub off on me. It never did but we became good friends and I think of you often.

'The Kellys': Penny, Des, Dan, Abby and Max 'the Guinea Killer!' You gave me a home in the true sense of the word. I am eternally grateful and I think the world of you all.

Bury Crew: Thanks for the many great times (which translates as parties, pub nights, club nights, etc!) we've had and the many yet to come. Still can't work out how that baby aged so quickly!

Jessie and Dan (Wot, another mention?!): Who really have 'been there'. Cheers! 'Ndice one!'

Everyone at KM: Thanks to you all for not only being great colleagues but good friends. Special thanks to JB, Mike, Sim, Tarns, Cathy and Jill who have to put up with me more than most.

(And finally . . .) My Hamners: Ralph, Magdalene and Rough 'n' Tumble. You're lovely!

INTRODUCTION

I was fifteen years old when I first became a Christian and looking back now I realise that I had no idea just what I was letting myself in for. I suppose it's all a bit like falling in love. At first it all seems so perfectly straightforward. You simply go with your feelings, ride that tidal wave of euphoria and walk around with a sickly grin on your face for weeks and weeks! But we all know that a good relationship doesn't just happen; it has to be worked at. So why do we think it can be any different with God?

There are sure to be good times and bad times, times when it's hard to hold on and times when we feel like we will never let go. Times when we feel so close and full of love we could burst and times when we feel desperate and alone. It's not easy but that's how a relationship develops – and that's how faith develops – in *Swings and Roundabouts*.

Now I've always been one of those people (and unfortunately one of those Christians) who, when offered two possible ways of doing something, has always chosen the wrong way first. Not out of any true evil, just ignorance, curiosity or plain old confusion. Hence, I am a firm believer in the philosophy that we can learn from our mistakes. After all, I've often had no option!

As you might guess then, the last eight years have been a little crazy at times. Prayer has often been my only way of dealing with being that most volatile of creatures: a teenage Christian.

I hope this collection of prayers, written over the last eight years, is not only relevant and comforting to those encountering the same situations and feelings as I have but I also hope that others, like me, will be able to look back in time with a smile. Why? Simple: because although the rides are all over the place, that is what makes them so much fun!

SHARON

Decisions

Decisions . . .
Lord, sometimes I really hate making decisions.
I don't mean everyday choices
     like what I should have for lunch,
     or what colour toothbrush I should buy.

I mean the big ones, Lord.
The ones that could transform
     my life.
The ones that could,
     without being too melodramatic,
     change everything I know
     and everything I love.

You see, Lord,
     it's quite a difficult time
     for me at the moment.
I've come to the end
     of the path.
A path I have walked
     since I was five years old.
You know the one, Lord,
     that path known as education.

Ever since I can remember,
     my life has been perfectly mapped out for me.
Any decisions I had to make were limited,
     and I always had some idea of the outcome.

But now?
Well, now it's some kind of mad open-season
     on the decisions front.
At the moment
     I am trying to decide, once and for all,
     which career I am going to pursue,

which hobbies I should take up,
and which,
of all the new people I have met,
I should choose as good friends.
Basically, Lord,
I am trying to find out which route
the next part of my life should take
It's not very easy, Lord.
In fact,
it's really quite intimidating.

Suddenly there are so many options to consider,
so many paths I could follow.
I mean, Lord,
how can I possibly choose between them?

I don't even know
where each path might lead.
There are so many possible far reaching consequences.
So many uncertainties.

I really wish
that you could provide me
with some kind of flow chart,
just something
which maps out
all the options I can choose from.
Something which shows exactly
where each decision will lead me.
That would make things so much easier, Lord,
don't you think?

As it is, Lord,
I feel like I am walking down a dark,
narrow alleyway.
There are no signs to even tell me
where I am now,
never mind where I am heading.

There aren't even any landmarks
    to give me a bit of a clue.
I really think that I might get lost here,
    it seems like drifting from the path,
    and making all the wrong decisions,
    would be really quite easy.

Maybe the best choice, Lord,
    would be to just not make any choices at all,
    to simply avoid all that decision making stuff
    and just let life happen to me.

Maybe if I take this attitude to life though, Lord,
    I will never get anywhere.
Perhaps I will just tread myself into a rut,
    and miss out on exciting experiences and people.

The truth is
    that I know that I must now move on,
    but it can be so worrying,
    making that first move.
I know how unreliable my own judgement can be,
    how unsound my own brainwaves and ideas are.
If I depend only on myself
    I know that I am sure to get lost.

So I turn to you, Lord.
Where should I go from here?
Which new challenges should I take up?
Who should I choose as my companions on the journey?

Guide me, Lord,
    on this new path.

Amen.

Told you so

Lord, I can hardly believe it!
You've done it again,
    you've really come through for me,
    just when I needed you most!

I really don't know how to thank you, Lord,
    I really don't know what to say at all.
For once in my life I am totally speechless!
Gob-smacked!

You would think that by now
    I would have realised
    that you always answer my prayers.
That you always listen to me whining on about things.
That you always help me out
    when I've gotten myself into trouble.
But this was really bolt out of the blue stuff, Lord.
Just like in the stories
    that I have heard other Christians
    tell me about.
You know God,
    those stories about miracles
    which always seem to happen to people
    who are much better Christians
    than I am.

It seems so simple when I think about it,
    and yet it's just so amazing;
I prayed,
    you answered,
    and not just in a whisper,
    but in a huge booming voice!

I had a problem,
	and you sorted it out.
WOW!

What more can I say, Lord?
How can I ever thank you?

I know I shouldn't be so surprised
	that you answered my prayer.
After all, that's what you do.
But the thing is, Lord,
I know that the situation I was in
	was all of my own doing,
As usual, I ignored all the advice
	and guidance
	you tried to give me,
	and went my own sweet way.
I paid no attention to the warning signs.
Then, when things started to go wrong
	I just couldn't understand it.
I started to question everything.
Perhaps I even blamed you
	for what was happening.

Despite this, Lord,
	you saw the state I was in,
	you saw what I had done to myself,
	and you took pity on me.
In one swift move you changed my whole world.
You whisked me away
	from all the turmoil and upset,
	picked me up off the floor
	where I had fallen
	and rearranged my messed up life
	into some kind of comprehensible order.
Then you set me down in a much nicer place;
	a place where you wanted me to be,

a place where I would have been all along
if only I had listened to you.

I thank you, Lord,
  for answering my prayers,
  even though I know that I don't deserve it.
Thank you for not giving up on me
  when I refuse to listen,
  when I trust only in my own fallible self.
Thank you for getting me out of the trouble
  I cause for myself.
Thank you for striving continually
  to make me see the light
  and not just abandoning me
  to the destiny I chose for myself.

Most of all Lord,
  thank you for not saying
  'I told you so!'

Amen.

King for a day

Lord, I see you riding into Jerusalem
    on the back of a donkey.
Around you there is a huge crowd of people,
    some of them pave your way with palm leaves,
    others are shouting for joy.
And here you are, entering the holy city,
    the city of God,
    the city of your father,
    just like a hero returning from war.

For years you have lived in poverty,
    even being born in a humble stable.
And for years you
    have carried out your ministry
    in virtual obscurity,
    only witnessing
    and preaching
    to those who seek you.
Now, finally,
    you are receiving the praise
    and recognition
    you really deserve.
How must you be feeling, Lord?
Like a king for a day?

But you knew that the 'alleluias' and admiration
    would be short lived.
Now I picture you hanging on that wooden cross.
The people who had once shouted in joy
    now shout, 'Crucify him!'
The people who had once laid palm leaves at your feet,
    now draw lots
    for your garments.
And yet, Lord, as you hang on that cross,
    with your hands and feet pierced by nails,

with your head crowned in thorns,
I can see that you are more majestic than any king,
you are more victorious than any war hero.
As I hear you utter triumphantly, 'it is finished'
I realise that you really do live up
to the title which is nailed above your head.
Once again
you are king for a day.

But, Lord, you knew that death could not hold you,
and now I see an empty cross,
a stone that has been rolled away,
and an empty tomb.
I can feel the joy of those who never lost faith in you,
I can feel the amazement of those who did.
For on this day, Lord, you have risen from the dead,
and you truly are king for a day.

I consider all that happened to you, Lord.
All the pain you must have felt on that cross
as you hung there
with the sin of the world
placed upon your shoulders;
your wounds bleeding,
your heart aching.

I consider the resurrection
and the promise of new and eternal life.
The hope you brought
into a world of sin.

I cry out to you, Lord,
and I ask you to be my king.
But not just for a day, Lord,
not for a week,
or month,

or year . . .
. . . but for every day of my life.

Lord,
I pray that one day
all people may come to understand
who you really are.
I pray that you might be recognised as king.
Not just a king of the Jews,
but a king for everybody,
the king who shall reign
in people's hearts
and minds.

Amen.

Wah, wah, wah

Wah, wah,
    wah, wah, wah . . .

I'm not boring you, am I, Lord?
Not going on too much?
Or perhaps talking for the sake of talking?

I do that sometimes, you know.
I get an idea in my head,
    something that I desperately need to say,
    something I'm convinced everyone else
    needs to hear . . .
And I go on about it . . .
    and on,
    and on,
    and on,
    and on,
    for quite some time.

The thing is,
    I know I don't just do it to my friends.
I do it to you, as well.

It's just that there are times
    when something is troubling me
    or preying on my mind
    and I really need to tell you about it.
To talk through my feelings,
    to let you know what I'm thinking.

Like you don't already know, God!
Like you can't actually read my every thought
    and every mood!

You are God!
You know everything!
So why do I feel the need to tell you?

Am I just babbling?
Is it that I need such an eventful life,
    with so many things
    happening to me.
So many things to 'wah, wah' about.

Or is it that I simply like
    talking to you.
Sharing my life.

And guess what . . .
    you know the answer!

Thanks, God . . .
    again.

Amen.

Dancing in puddles

Lord,
    I am alone,
    walking down a quiet street,
    watched only by the moonlight.
The amber glow of the street lamp
    turning the rain drops
    into melting honey
    as they rain down
    onto the tarmac.

It smears my make-up,
    flattens my hair,
    drenches my clothes . . .

    . . . and it's brilliant!

It's at times like these
    that the only care I have
    is the smile on my face!
A wide,
    cheery,
    smile!
Brimming with happiness,
    as my eyes glint
    with childhood glee.

I hold my head up,
    my face to the falling rain
    as it lands on my cheeks.

It splashes, cold
    and soothing.
It washes over me
    like a river or contentment,
    filling my mind

with memories of childhood,
when worries were far away.

Then,
from the corner of my eye,
I see it.

Mischief takes over,
adulthood takes a back seat (yay!)
then I break into a run,
laughing as I go,
and leap,
with both impractically-clad feet,
into a pool
of splashing,
splishing,
sploshing,
heaven!

The water cascades around me,
as I kick it,
and splash it,
and dance on the face of the moon,
reflected in it.

Lord,
so often life seems to rain down on me.
With all it's troubles
and concerns.

Please help me to lift my head to turn on that smile,
that mischievous grin,
and go dancing
through the rush of everyday life,
in just the same way
that I dance now,
through the puddles.

Amen.

Fear of the Spirit

Oh, God,
>what's going on?
What is happening here?
It's all so scary
>and confusing.
To be honest, God,
>it's just downright weird.

All around me
>people are falling to the floor
>collapsing in heaps,
>jerking violently,
>muscles twitching,
>eyes flickering.
Bodies slain alright . . .
>but by what?
By the 'Spirit'?
In the 'Spirit'?
In *your* 'Spirit'?

And the noise, Lord.
The shrieking laughter
>which pierces the air.
The mumbling
>and murmuring.
People speaking in a thousand languages,
>a thousand different tongues.

Lord,
>none of this makes any sense,
>not to me, anyway.
Just out of interest
>(and to prove that I actually do
>read the Bible . . . occasionally!)
>where is the interpreter?

The person who can translate these sounds,
    these strange events,
    into something I can understand?

I feel so alone,
    separated from the crowd.
By my lack of understanding,
    and by my fear of the unknown.

Am I just stupid?
Not seeing what lies
    before my own two eyes?
A doubting Thomas?
Refusing to believe?
Too scared to believe?
Perhaps I am just inadequate.
A third rate Christian.
My soul being far too soiled,
    far too unclean,
    for your spirit
    to enter.

Is that why I must now play
    'odd one out'?
Is that why I now stand alone,
    unaffected;
    an obvious beacon
    of stupidity
    for all to see?

Am I really so bad,
    that even you
    are unable to love me?

Deep down, Lord,
    I know this is not true.
    I know you love me.

You see,
     I felt you calling,
     touching,
     trying to get through to me.
But I pushed you away,
     asked you to leave me.

Why, Lord?
Why?

Because I was scared.
Really, truly,
     frightened,
     of your Spirit.

And in the midst of all this mayhem,
     this is the only thing
     which really does not make sense.
How could I possibly fear
     your Spirit;
A Spirit of love?

Lord,
     help me to understand.
Take away this anxiety,
     this confusion,
     so that I too
     may open my heart to you,
     and speak to you
     in my own way.

Amen.

Woah, there!

God,
      I'm sure temptation shouldn't feel like this.
I'm sure it shouldn't feel so great,
      so, well,
      tempting!

It just doesn't fit in
      with what I'm used to.
What I've experienced before.
I thought temptation was meant
      to make you feel bad.
At least a little bit naughty.
I thought it was at least
      meant to be obvious.

But this is different.
The boundaries are so unclear.
The lines so blurred.
So normal.
Not like 'temptation' at all.

You see, Lord,
      I can't see how evil
      can come from love.
Who would it hurt?
How could it be wrong?

'Making Love' is surely just that,
      with no mention of hate
      or hurt,
      or humiliation,
      or ill health,
      or any of the usual consequences
      which come out of succumbing
      to temptation.

It's all so confusing!
(No surprise there, then!)

You do understand,
        don't you, Lord?
I know I'm probably just going on and on again,
        (wah, wah, wah . . .)
But I need to talk to you,
        feel you close.
These choices I have to make,
        the consequences . . .
All of it seems a bit too unreal.

Help me with this, Lord.
I know it's only one of a thousand problems
        that I'm bound to bore you with,
        but just to know you're there,
        listening,
        guiding,
        is a help.

Help me, Lord,
        to have only one temptation.
The temptation that,
        no matter what is happening,
        what I am doing,
I will always
        want to talk
        to you!

Amen.

Opium of the people?

Could it be, Lord?
Is it all just a lie?
An elaborate
    and cleverly crafted
    conspiracy?
The 'Opiate' of the masses.
That's what the lecturer said, Lord.
That's how he described religion.
Again and again, he quoted the words of Karl Marx.
He said that religion is just a tool
    created to control society.
Used by the ruling classes
    to maintain the status quo.

What were his exact words, Lord?
'It dulls the pain of oppression
    and makes life bearable'.
It stops the working classes
    from realising their true situation.
From seeing the true state
    of poverty
    and oppression
    in which they live.
Thus preventing them
    from uprising against those in power.

Well, it does seem possible, doesn't it, Lord?
Just look at all the rules
    attached to Christianity.
Rules which govern and control
The whole emphasis
    that is placed on the next life.

An emphasis
        which is perhaps intended
        to stop people
        looking too closely
        at this life.

Lord,
        there is so much evidence
        to support this theory.
Could it possibly be true?
I really don't want it to be, Lord.
I hate the thought
        that everything upon which I have based my life
        is a lie.
Simply an institution
        created to control me.

But what evidence have you offered
        in return?
What solid proof do I have
        that my relationship with you,
        my faith in you,
        is not just something
        my mind has created.
A concept I've latched onto
        to fulfil my need,
        to believe that there is
        'something out there'.
Something more,
        a meaning to my existence.

I've never even seen you, Lord,
        or physically felt you.
I have never spoken in tongues,
        been slain in the Spirit,
        heard your voice . . .

But it's not supposed to be easy, is it?
After all,
  if you came down here
  in all your power
  we'd be so scared
  that the idea of a one to one relationship
  would be out the window.

Which isn't what you want.
You want us to return the love
  you have for us
  as best we can.
To have a relationship
  that relies on faith,
  love,
  trust.
Not power.

Perhaps, Lord,
  it is doubt
  that is the Opium of masses.
That nagging feeling that the truth
  you give us
  by being a loving God
  isn't actually real.
That we are kidding ourselves.

Where, in fact,
  it is the one thing real enough,
  and big enough,
  to sustain us for eternity.

Thanks, Lord.

Amen.

At peace

Peace ripples through my heart,
    trickles through my soul
    and laps along the edges of my mind.

Love radiates through my body,
    warms my spirit
    and shines golden
    onto my face.

Happiness chirps in my ears,
    coos through my smile,
    and warbles in contented tones
    in my head.

Lord,
    even though the storms of life
    rage about me.
Even though the troubles
    spill down on the path ahead,
    summer remains in my heart,
    mind and soul,
    because that is where you dwell, Lord.

Amen.

Buzzin'

Lord,
> what a feeling!
What a wonderful feeling!

Walking on sunshine,
> floating on a cloud,
> riding the wave of life!
Hyper,
> high,
> rushin',
> buzzin'!

It feels so good to be alive today, Lord.
So good to be me.
I'm so happy,
> so filled with excitement
> about tomorrow.
This is fantastic!

I'm totally and utterly happy!
And why do I feel like this?
Why do I feel like I do?
Is it drugs?
Have I been drinking?
Popping pills?
Fallen in love?

Nope . . .

Made a new friend?
Found a new job?
Been given a promotion?
Passed an exam?

Nope . . .

It can't be.
To feel this good
it would have to be all the above
and so much more.

So what about
rushing with adrenalin,
parachuting,
or bungy jumping,
or climbing,
or skiing?

No, Lord,
this high is far too sustained,
persistent,
permanent.

No, Lord,
I know why
I am so high.

I'm filled with the spirit of you.
Filled with your love.

How many times
have I found it impossible to cry?
Yet now, the tears of joy
roll freely
down my cheeks.
Washing away all the hurt
in one huge tidal wave
of happiness!

It's brilliant, Lord!
Thanks!

Amen.

Free

Lord,
    I feel so free.
All my life
    I have been trapped
    within my insecurities.
Confined
    by my lack of confidence,
    and now you have come along.

You've loosened the chains,
    broken the shackles,
    freed me from my prison.

You called me to step out in faith
    whilst I was so reluctant,
    so scared
    of what may lay ahead.
Afraid of the unknown world
    you wanted me to enter.

But for once in my life
    I trusted you.
I placed my life and career
    totally in your hands.
I actually did your will.
I made the biggest step
    of my life
    and I did it for you.

It really wasn't easy, Lord.
There were so many times
    I questioned whether I was doing the right thing.
So many times
    I doubted you.

You were asking me to give up so much.
You were asking me to leave behind loved ones,
    very dear friends
    and a lot of precious memories.

You were asking me
    to move into an unknown area.
To start a new job,
    make new friends,
    find a new home.

So many changes
    and in such a little time.
So many things
    I really didn't think I could do.
But, Lord,
    you helped me all the way.
You supported my every step.
You held me up
    when I was weak.
Calmed me down
    when I was upset.

I came to you
    in my times of need
    and you provided
    in abundance.

My family and friends
    did their best to help me.
They were all there for me.

I've found a quiet confidence
    I never knew I had.

Out of my dependence on you
    and loved ones,
    has sprung a unique independence.

I feel so free,
    so alive,
    so excited by a life
    that now offers so much
    for me to take advantage of.
Opportunities I had never conceived before.

The world is my oyster,
    and I am free to take advantage of it!

Thank you, Lord!

Amen.

Staring at the sky

I stare at the sky;
    at an expanse of blackness
    broken only by pinpricks
    of ancient light.
An entire universe
    is hanging above my head.
Billions and billions
    of stars and planets
    which reach far beyond my comprehension.
It's a beautiful
    and scary sight.

There is so much in this world
    that I will never see.
So much I will never know.
And yet this world
    could be just one of many
    hanging in this huge expanse.

An expanse with no walls,
    no end,
    truly infinite.

Sometimes I feel so small,
    so insignificant.
I'm just a mere blip
    on the world's surface.

I can't help wondering
    about the point of my life.
Why do I exist?
For that matter, Lord,
    why do *any* of us exist?
What is the meaning of *anyone's* life?

I consider 'forever'.
The 'forever' that you know, Lord.
The 'forever' that you've seen.
The billions of years
    which have shaped the planet I live on.
The years which have built mountains
    and moved continents.

I realise that my existence
    on this planet
    represents only a twinkling
    of an eye,
    a mere spark
    in time.
The world
    was here long before
    my arrival.
And it will be here
    long after
    I leave.

I am nothing,
    nobody;
    just another pawn
    in the game of life.

Yet, Lord,
    you know who I am,
    you know everything about me,
    and you love me.
Not just a little,
    but enough
    to actually die for me.

But who am I
    that you should even know my name,
    let alone be my friend,
    my father,
    my saviour?

Yet even more that this, Lord.
I actually exist
    because you want me to,
    because you created me!

And I realise that my life does have a meaning,
    that there is a point to my existence.
The meaning is you, Lord.
The meaning of everything,
    is you.

So now I look once again at the sky,
    and I thank you.
I thank you
    for creating me.
I thank you
    for loving me.
And I thank you
    for making me a part
    of your wonderful universe.

Amen.

'O Lord, what is man that you care for him,
the Son of Man that you think of him?
Man is like a breath,
his days are like a fleeting shadow.'

(Psalm 144:3 and 4)

'When I consider your heavens,
the work of your fingers,
the moon and the stars,
which you have set in place.
What is man that you are mindful of him,
the Son of Man that you care for him?
You made him a little lower than the heavenly beings
and crowned with the glory and honour.'

(Psalm 8:3-5)

I believe

How do I get through the bad times,
    when the sun won't shine at all?
How do I get through the heartache
    when I feel so broken and small?

How do I get through the long days
    when every step is a trial?
How do I deal with rejection
    whilst crying, just like a child?

How do I face all my fears
    when I feel so weak and alone?
How do I find my happiness
    when all I want is to moan?

How do I deal with the hurting
    when my broken heart won't mend?
How do I find any comfort
    when I cannot find a friend?

How do I deal with the failure
    when success seems so near yet so far?
How do I get through the bad times
    and in darkness look for the star?

I believe in God my father
    and the love he offers all.
I believe in Christ my saviour;
    he will never let me fall.

I believe . . .

Amen.

Post-teen crisis

Lord, here I am;
        21 years old!
And just look at my life.
My dull, drab,
        boring life.

What have I done with it?
What have I done
        with all the wonderful gifts
        and opportunities
        you have given me?
What have I managed to achieve?
What impact
        has my existence
        had on anything?

Well, I'll tell you, Lord.
NOTHING!
I have done nothing with my life.
I have done nothing
        with all the gifts
        and opportunities
        you have given me.
I have achieved nothing.
A big, fat, zero.

I've just sat back
and watched,
        as so many things
        in my life
        have just come and gone.
So many people,
        so many opportunities,
        and I've just never put in

that little bit of extra effort
which might have made things
so different.

I mean, Lord,
    just look at all the hobbies I've had.
Everything from rock climbing
        to dancing,
        from playing in wind bands
        to joining fitness clubs.
        and yet I've never stuck at any of them!
I've never managed to excel
        at anything.
I'm a true Jack of all trades
        and master of none.

Look at all the wonderful friends I have had.
        People who have helped me through difficult
        times,
        people who have made me laugh,
        people who have had an important influence on
        my life.
So where are they now?

It seems that I've been given plenty of gifts, Lord,
        plenty of opportunities,
        and all I seem to have done
        is waste them.

Where does that leave me now, Lord?
What am I doing with my life?
What do I stand for?
What do I believe?
What am I?
Who am I?

Another cog in the wheel?
Another brick in the wall?
Insignificant,
      unimportant.
Little miss average?

Where do I go from here, Lord?
What do I want to do?
What am I capable of achieving?
Who do I want to be?

I just feel
      like I have been totally immersed
      in drab, daily routine,
      in just trying to get by,
      in just trying to keep my head
      above the water.

I feel unchallenged,
      uninspired,
      bored.
And the worst of it is,
      I have only myself to blame.

Oh, Lord,
      there is so much I long for.
I long to be someone special.
I long to achieve something great.
I long for my existence to make a difference.
I long for the excitement of a challenge.
I long for an aim and a purpose.

I really want to be different, Lord,
      to be, in some way, a significant member
      of the human race.
So please, Lord,
      help me to do something with my life.
Help me to do something worthwhile

with the gifts and opportunities
you give me.
Don't let me sit here any longer
and just watch
as my life passes me by.

Help me to break out of my daily routines
and accept the challenges
you offer.
Help me to make
some kind of valuable contribution
to the world I live in.
Help me to actually make something of my life.

Please, Lord!

Amen.

'For I know the plans I have for you,' declares the Lord, 'plans to
prosper you and not to harm you, plans to give you hope and a
future.'

(Jeremiah 29:11)

I did it!

Lord,
    I'm only 5′ 2″,
    I'm not particularly broad
    or strong,
    but sometimes
    I feel like the load
    you place on my shoulders
    is just too much
    to bear.
More than I can take.

So many times
    you put me through
    the mill,
    allowing me
    and my faith
    to be tested
    over,
    and over,
    again.

So often I feel
    like I'm quickly approaching
    breaking point,
    where the pain cuts deeply
    when I can see no way out,
    when I cry out to you in desperation.

I know I sound melodramatic, Lord,
    but you've got to admit
    you've thrown
    some pretty harsh stuff
    my way.

At the tender age of 22
    I can say
    that I grew up with bulimia,
    coped (only just)
    as my mum battled with cancer,
    and my grandma fought back
    after a huge heart attack
    (apparently having the strength of a lion
    runs in the family!)

I have seen two friends
    brush death's door
    after overdosing on drugs,
    lived in an area
    where riots and burglars
    were common day occurrences,
    but where sleeping soundly
    and feeling safe, however,
    were not.

And I've had my fair share
    of heartbreaks,
    failed relationships,
    betrayals,
    guilts,
    and disappointments.

Not surprisingly then, Lord,
    'Why me?' is a phrase
    which commonly leaves my lips.

And yet, Lord,
    at the tender age of 22,
    I can also say,
    that I did it.
    I made it through.

You tested me,
    and my faith
    and here I am now
    to tell the tale.

A stronger,
    happier,
    more determined person
    than ever I was before,
    having achieved
    so much more
    than I would ever have conceived,
    knowing I am capable
    of much more to come.

The only reason
    any of this is so,
    the reason
    why I have this new strength
    is because you
    have allowed me
    to suffer.

So, as strange as it may sound, Lord,
    thank you,
    for the suffering,
    and the testing.

Amen.

Why, Lord?

Lord,
     why?
Why do you allow us to suffer?
How can you watch
     as all these terrible things happen
     to the people you love,
     the people you created.
Why don't you intervene, Lord?
Do something to ease the pain?

Every day our TVs
     flash pictures of war,
     famine,
     fatal accidents,
     natural disasters.
The faces of their victims
     tell tales of desperation,
     devastation,
     and fear.

Don't you love us any more?
Don't you care?
Have you forsaken us,
     grown tired of all the evil we do and say,
     and abandoned us to ourselves?

I wouldn't blame you if you had done, Lord.
I know we must frustrate you
     and hurt you.
You probably think we're just a lost cause,
     too far gone to ever be saved.

But, Lord,
     I really cannot believe
     that you would ever leave us,

or that you could simply turn your back,
in spite of all we do.

In the midst of all this suffering
I can still feel you near,
your love in my heart.
I can see the many things
you do in peoples lives.
In my life.

So, tell me, Lord,
if you are still with us,
why do you allow us to suffer?
Is it you who inflicts the pain?
Who causes the hurt?
Are you trying to punish us for all that we do wrong?
Paying us back for our sin?
Teaching us the error of our ways?

I know that we must anger you,
that we need to be chastised,
that we deserve to be punished.
But Lord,
I also know that you love us,
and so I am sure that must hate
to see our suffering.
Like a father loves his children,
you could never be the one
to inflict the pain.

If this is the case,
then, Lord,
I ask again,
why do you allow people to suffer?

Are you testing us?
Are you trying to find out how strong our faith is?
Pushing us as hard as you can
just to see if we will crack?

To see whether we are worthy of your love?
Is this some kind of exam
    that we must pass
    is order to gain entry to your kingdom?

It would certainly make sense.
We all know how easy it is to be a Christian
    when all is going well.
When being a Christian
    means that you can have a better life.
After all, if being a Christian was always easy,
    guaranteeing freedom from suffering,
    then everyone would do it!

Real Christian strength
    comes from having faith
    when the odds are against you,
    when you have 1001 reasons to doubt.

But, even if suffering
    simply was a test,
    this would still mean
    that it would be you, Lord,
    who caused us to suffer.
You who inflicted hurt and pain.
And this is something
    which I cannot
    and do not
    believe.
That a loving God,
    could possibly do.

So, Lord,
    I'm afraid the question remains.
WHY?
Why, Lord?
Why do you allow your people to suffer?

Amen.

The grip of sin

Sin, Lord.
Could it be that I live constantly
    in the grip of sin?
It feels like that sometimes.
As though sinning is all I ever do.
From the minute I wake
    to the moment I finally drop off to sleep.

Why is it, Lord?
Why is it that everything I do,
    everything I ever think
    always seems to be the wrong thing?

It's not that I don't know wrong from right,
    and it's not that I don't know how to be good.
I really wish I had those excuses.

It's just that so often
    being bad
    seems so much more exciting,
    so much more interesting,
    than being good.

Isn't that a terrible thing to admit, Lord?
Doesn't that make me a terrible Christian?
A horrible person?

Sometimes I feel as though
    sin is this huge hand
    that holds me.
Its fingers are wrapped around my throat,
    its nails into my flesh.

Sometimes it just won't seem to let go
    and it's only afterwards,
    when sin has relaxed its suffocating grip,
    that I really think about what I have done,
    about the things I have said,
    the thoughts I've had,
    the hurt I've caused.

Then, of course,
    I am so often filled with regret,
    with guilt,
    with remorse . . .

    . . . and I come to you, Lord,
    begging for your forgiveness,
    vowing to never repeat
    what I have done,
    wishing I had never done it
    in the first place.

But, to my relief,
    you take me into your loving arms
    and forgive me.
Taking away all my guilt and hurt
    no matter how bad I have been.

So I start anew,
    full of good intentions,
    brimming with firm resolutions,
    determined to change,
    to be different.

But before I know it,
    temptation strikes again,
    curls its fingers around me once more.

Lord,
        help me to break free.
To wriggle out
        of this suffocating
        situation,
        and to instead
        take hold of your guiding hand
        which will lead me around
        the pitfalls of life.

Amen.

We know that the law is spiritual;
but I am unspiritual, sold as a slave to sin . . .

I know that nothing good lives in me,
that is, in my sinful nature. For I have
the desire to do what is good,
but I cannot carry it out. For what I do
is not the good I want to do; no, the evil
I do not want to do – this I keep on doing . . .

What a wretched man I am! Who will rescue me
from this body of death? Thanks be to God – through
Jesus Christ our Lord!

(Romans 7:14-25)

It's not fair!

Oh, God, why is life so unfair?
Why is it so unfair to me?

I mean,
    take my A levels for example.
Now I know I could have tried a lot harder,
    and I know I could have done
    a lot more revision,
    but I did work throughout the year,
    I never missed lectures
    and I always got good grades.
So how come those people who never attended lectures
    did so much better than me?
How come people who did less revision than me
    managed to get better marks?
It just doesn't seem fair to me, God.
Is there no justice?

Take my appearance
    as another example.
I mean, I really do try to make the best of myself,
I try everything I can
    to make myself look good.
I exercise regularly,
    I look after my skin and hair,
    and I've even had braces
    to straighten my teeth.
Where has it got me?
Absolutely nowhere.

How come so many other people
    are just born beautiful?
They never have to put
    any effort in at all,
    and yet they always look so stunning.
How can that possibly be fair?

And what about my career prospects?
Why should people be advising me
    to lie in job interviews
    about whether I have got a boyfriend,
    just because potential employers
    might assume
    that I'm going to want children
    in the near future,
    something which would, of course,
    make me an unwise investment.
    And yet men are simply assessed
    at face value.
Men are simply evaluated
    on their achievements
    and qualifications,
    and rarely even asked
    about their home life.
Now where is the justice in that?

Oh, God, there is so much in this world
    that I don't understand.
But most of all,
    I don't understand
    why this world is so unfair.
I don't just mean the minor injustices
    that I have experienced.

You see, Lord,
    I look around me,
    at the world I live in,
    and all I see is injustice.

I see people
    who are being discriminated against
    every day.
In the workplace,
    in politics,
    even in the street,
    just because they are a different race
    or a different colour
    from the majority.

I see people with hang-ups,
    people with psychological problems,
    people who are in dead-end jobs,
    people who are unemployed
    or homeless,
    and people who are in prison,
    just because as children
    they were given
    a bad start in life.

I see people
    who are being denied things
    that so many others
    just take for granted.
Like clean water,
    food to eat,
    health care
    and education,
    basic rights,
    just because they were born
    into a poor country.

And, God,
    this is just the tip of the iceberg.
There are so many
    who must suffer
    through no fault of their own.

Then, on the other side of the coin
    there are the privileged.
People who revel in luxury and wealth.
People with power,
    people with money,
    people who do nothing
    but abuse what they have been given.

Why is life like this?
Surely this is not your will.
It's just not fair!

Amen.

So angry!

Lord,
    I am so angry.
I'm absolutely livid!
I just despair at this world!

I cannot believe
    how multinationals
    can be allowed to exploit
    the people and resources
    of the third world
    in order to put money
    in the pockets
    of their share holders.
Native peoples
    are stripped of their lands
    and livelihoods,
    left to starve.
    and people die of preventable diseases.

I can't understand
    how some business owners
    can get away with exploiting
    and mistreating their work force
    in order to maximise profits
    whilst many struggle
    to pay their bills
    and mortgages,
    living with the daily dread
    that they may become unemployed
    or homeless.

Lord,
    how can politicians
    have so little conscience

that they can lie and scheme
in a desperate attempt
to further their own careers,
when major groups in our society
are denied any political voice,
big business
pollutes our environment,
and racist groups
continue their reign of fear.

I despair at how murderers,
    rapists and thieves
    go about satisfying
    their own warped desires,
    robbing people of their sense of security.
Leaving them as victims
    to pick up the broken pieces
    of their lives.

Lord,
    I wish these cases were the exception,
    but they are not.
They are the rule.

How can people be so cold hearted?
So callous?
So selfish?
So many people have abandoned
    the whole idea
    of loving others.
Abandoned the whole idea
    of doing unto others
    as they would have done
    unto themselves.
Instead, people seem to be preoccupied
    with doing unto others
    whatever they can get away with.

Doing unto others
     before they can be done unto
     in the same way.

Lord, why is this?
Why is the world so evil?
What can I do
     to make this world
     any better?
What can anybody do?

Lord, I really am so angry.
And if I am angry,
then, Lord,
just how angry are you?

Amen.

'O righteous God,
who searches minds and hearts,
bring to an end the violence of the wicked
and make the righteous secure.'
(Psalm 7:9)

For the least of these

Lord,
> if I had met your mother and Joseph in Bethlehem,
> homeless,
> hungry,
> and tired,
> would I have offered them a room?
Given them something to eat?
Found somewhere for you to be born?
Given all that I could
> to welcome you
> into the world?

Or would I have turned them away?
Told them
> that there was no room for them to stay?
Said that there was no spare food?
Told them
> that I had nowhere for you to be born?

What if I had been a shepherd
> guarding my sheep,
> or a wise man
> studying the stars;
> would I have dropped everything
> to go in search of you?
Travelled for miles
> to see you?
Placed my trust in the words
> of an angel,
or the movement of the stars,
in order to find you?

Or would I have stayed just where I was?
Considered my job far too important
        to just up and leave?
Argued that the journey was too long
        and arduous?
Doubted the visions
        I had seen?

And when you were older, Lord,
        what if I had witnessed
        one of your many miracles,
        or heard one of your great stories or sermons.
Would I have believed my own eyes?
Placed my faith in you?
Heeded your words?
Trusted in your divine wisdom?
Given up all I had to follow you?
Believed you were the Son of God?

Or would I have discounted
        the things I had seen
        as tricks or works of the devil?
Criticised your sermons?
Mocked you and called you an impostor?
Hailed to see who you were?

Lord, what if I had seen your trial?
Would I have shouted for them to crucify you?
Abandoned you
        in your time of need?
Forsaken you
        and denied that you were ever
        my friend and saviour?

What about on the day of your crucifixion, Lord?
Would I have helped you to carry your cross?
Offered you a drink to quench my thirst?

Stood by you to the end?

Or would I have jeered you and mocked you?
Cast lots for your clothes?
Placed a crown of thorns on your head?

Lord, I hope and pray
that I would have always stood by you.
That I would have done anything for you,
even given my life for you,
as you did for me.

But, Lord,
every day I see people around me
who need my support:
the homeless,
the exploited,
the grieving,
the lonely,
the starving.

Lord,
what do I do for any of these?
What do I do for the people you love?

Do I offer my home to them?
Fight for their rights?
Comfort them in their times of need?
Befriend them?
Offer them food?

So often, Lord,
the answer to these questions is 'no'.
So often I have the opportunity
to help someone,
so often I just don't bother.
I really don't think

it's because I am really a bad person,
just that to help, sometimes
takes a little too much effort.
Just a little more care
and love
than I am prepared to give.

Sometimes, Lord,
the temptation to be lazy and uncaring
is just too strong.
And yet, Lord,
your words ring in my ears,
and I remember that what I do
for the least of these people,
I do for you.

Please, Lord,
help me to learn.
Help me to show other people
the same love and care
that I hope I would have shown you,
if I had met you when you lived on earth as a man.
Please use me, Lord,
as a window for your love
to shine through,
so that the people I meet
might come to know you
in the way I do.

Amen.

In glass houses

Oh, God,
>it's so easy to be the one
>to cast stones.

To see the splinter
>in someone else's eye.

To apply harsh measures
>in judging other people.

So often I criticise people
>for the things they do.

I get angry
>about their lack of concern
>for fellow human beings,
>so arrogant in my belief
>that 'they' are doing wrong.

And yet, God,
>I ask you to be lenient with me,
>to be understanding,
>to be forgiving.

So often I ask you to apply soft measures
>when it comes to judging
>my own actions.

To ignore the plank
>which resides in my own eye,
>because the truth is
>that I do a lot of things
>which I know must anger you.

Things which must hurt
>other people.

Things for which I
>should be judged harshly.

Yet I can be so self-righteous.

God, all of a sudden I am scared,
>I'm very scared indeed.

You see, it has finally dawned on me
just how judgmental I can be.
Deep down I know that the measures I use,
the stones I cast,
will one day be aimed
at me.

Surely, Lord,
if I am to be judged
as severely as I have judged others
then there is no hope.
No way I will ever be forgiven.
No way I'll ever make it to heaven.

You see, God,
it's all very well me complaining
about the state of this world,
it's all very well me saying
that I am surrounded by evil,
but the truth is that the only evil
I am surrounded by
is of my own making.

We all sin!
It might be a sad admission
but it's a fact.
We are all human,
and we all fall short
of the standards
that you have set us.

But you are a merciful God,
you forgive us our sins
and give us the chance
to start again;
over,
and over,
and over again.

So what gives me the right
to pass judgement?

What gives me the right
    to be so unforgiving?
Me!
A sinner in my own right!

I live in a glass house.
A very fragile glass house.
How can I possibly throw stones?

After all,
    only you have the right to judge,
    and one day you will judge me.

I pray, Lord,
    that by then
    I will have learnt
    to be less judgmental,
    learnt to be more forgiving
    and understanding,
    learnt to concentrate
    on putting my own life
    in order.

Because I know
    that my forgiveness
    depends on your leniency,
    that my salvation
    depends on your great mercy
    and love.

    Amen.

'For if you forgive men when they sin against you,
your heavenly Father will also forgive you.
But if you do not forgive men their sins,
your father will not forgive your sins.'
(Matthew 6:14 and 15)

'Do not judge, or you too will be judged.
For in the same way as you judge others, you will be judged,
and with the measure you use, it will be measured to you.'
(Matthew 7:1 and 2)

I am

Lord,
    I am loud,
    demonstrative,
    boisterous,
    lairy,
    mad,
    adventurous,
    brave,
    enthusiastic.

I am shy,
    under confident,
    self conscious,
    and scared.

I am bored,
    unimpressed,
    fed up,
    and down.

I am loyal,
    faithful,
    supportive,
    kind,
    patient,
    peaceful,
    hard working
    and intelligent.

I am loving,
    caring,
    giving,
    and sharing.

I am selfish,
     self centred,
     thoughtless,
     lazy,
     daft,
     sinful
     and stupid.

I'm so many things.
Some good,
     some bad.

All of it
     is me.

Thank you, Lord,
     for making me this way.

Amen.

Laughter

Lord,
  we laughed so hard
  that our eyes vanished,
  our bellies ached,
  and we could hardly breathe.

It was a simple joke.
Not cruel,
  or dirty,
  or complicated.
Just a childish joke.

I can't even recall it now.
Something about elephants and trees.
Something bizarre and absurd.

But I remember clearly
  that wonderful sound.
The wonderful feeling.
The pure enjoyment
  and happiness shared.
Even as I replay the events
  in my mind.

It brings a smile to my face
  and I chuckle insanely to myself
  in the midst of my everyday life.

We managed to give each other
  one of the greatest gifts
  there ever was.

Our spirits were lifted,
  our lives were brightened.
There was a ray of sunshine.

Thank you, Lord,
  for the ache in my side,
  my gasps for air . . .

    . . . thank you for laughter.

Amen.